JOHNNY APPLESEED

John Chapman was his real name, but no one ever called this man anything but Johnny Appleseed. Here is his story, told so simply and skillfully that any young reader who has mastered a second grade reading vocabulary can read it by himself.

Massachusetts was Johnny's home, but he traveled West into the Ohio territory to plant his apple seeds all over the countryside and to care for the trees. He was never afraid of the Indians, for they knew he was their friend. In the springtime, when the young apple trees bloomed, the lonely settlers in the wilderness remembered Johnny Appleseed's visit. In the autumn, when the trees were loaded with ripe fruit, they were grateful to him. When Johnny was too old to go on planting seeds, he went to live with the many friends he had made. People came to visit him and he told them about the old days, when he started out with a sack on his back, and no shoes on his feet.

JOHNNY APPLESEED

By Gertrude Norman

Illustrated by James Caraway

A SEE AND READ

Beginning to Read Biography

G. P. PUTNAM'S SONS   NEW YORK

Twelfth Impression

SBN: GB 399-60323-9

© 1960 by Gertrude Norman
Illustrations © 1960 by James Caraway
Library of Congress Catalog Card Number: 60-12531
Manufactured in the United States of America
Published simultaneously in the Dominion of Canada
by Longmans, Green and Company, Toronto.
07209

Once there was a boy and his name was Johnny Chapman. Johnny was a happy boy. He lived on a farm and he liked the outdoors—woods, birds, animals. Best of all, he liked the apple trees that grew on his father's farm.

Soon Johnny knew how to plant seeds
to grow more trees, and to care for the
trees he planted.

When Johnny grew up, he liked to go
and stay in the woods. He did not take a
gun, for he would not hurt any animal.

One night when the rain came down, he went to sleep in a log. Then he felt something soft next to him. It was a little bear. "I will not hurt you," said Johnny. "You are safe with me." And the bear stayed with him all night.

When he was twenty years old, Johnny went far away from the town where he grew up. He walked for days with a sack of apple seeds on his back. He wanted to plant the seeds in the wilderness.

At that time—many years ago, families went to live out west, in the wilderness. There in the deep woods, every town was far from the next town. Every house was far from the next house. Every family was far from the next family.

The families had to work hard from morning to night. There were logs to be cut, and animals to care for. It was hard to find food.

"I will go and plant seeds," said Johnny. "Then apple trees will grow, and there will be food for the folks who live in the wilderness."

Johnny would walk for many days
and see nothing but trees, birds, and
animals. But he liked the outdoors. He
was happy.

Sometimes he met an Indian. Then he made friends with the Indian. They would walk along for a bit or stop to cook dinner over a fire.

"Where are your gun and your shoes, White Man?" the Indian would ask.

"I get along fine," said Johnny, "without gun and shoes."

As Johnny walked in the woods one day, it began to snow. All day long the snow came down until it was very deep. Johnny was cold. He did not know what to do, for he knew he would have to walk for days to get to any house. "How can I walk without shoes," he said, "in the deep, deep snow?"

That night he made a fire and went
to sleep in a log. But the next morning,
the snow was still coming down. Now all
his food was gone. He had nothing to eat,
nothing but nuts from the trees.

"What can I do?" he said. "I can't stay here in the woods. I am lost and very cold."

Then he cut off a bit of his coat and put it around his feet. He took a branch from a tree and put it over the fire. That made the branch very soft. He cut it up and made snowshoes. Now he could walk in the snow.

At last, after many cold days, he came
to a house. An old woman lived there and
she was glad to see him.

He cut logs and took care of the cow and helped her around the house. He stayed until the last snow was gone and the days were fine and sunny again. Then he planted some seeds for her and said, "I'll come back some day."

Johnny was happy as he went on his way. He thought about the trees he would plant, all the pretty apple trees. They would make others happy, too.

Soon people began to talk of this man who walked along with a sack on his back. They liked to see Johnny as he stopped, to plant some seeds, and help other people when he could.

One morning he stopped at a house
and a little girl came to the door.

"What is in that sack?" she asked.

"Apple seeds," said Johnny.

"What good are seeds?" she said.
"Why not throw them away?"

"No," said Johnny, "I'll plant some
near your house, and one day you are
going to see a pretty apple tree."

Then the girl's mother came out.
"Why, I know who you are," she said. "Is
your name Johnny Appleseed?"

"Yes. That is what they call me now.
Once I had another name. It was Johnny
Chapman. Well—I like Appleseed best."

No one knew Johnny Chapman, but everyone knew Johnny Appleseed. Year-in, year-out, he went from town to town, from house to house.

Now more people lived in the wilderness and there had to be more food for them. The new little trees that Johnny first planted were big trees now with a lot of apples.

Folks were glad when he came to town. He showed them how to care for the trees, and he made a lot of friends everywhere he went.

But at the time when Johnny lived, many white men and Indians were not friends. First the Indians lived in the wilderness. Then the white men came and made them go away. Sometimes Indians and white men would fight. But Johnny would not fight. He would not hurt anyone.

Once, when Johnny came near a town, someone told him, "The Indians are hiding back of the hill. They are going to take the white men by surprise."

Johnny ran as fast as he could. He stopped at every house in the woods, shouting, "Run! Run! Hurry!" All day and all night he ran, shouting, "Run! Hurry! The Indians are hiding back of the hill. Run to the big house and you will be safe."

Then every father and mother took the children and ran to the big house. There the Indians could not hurt them.

After that, people liked to tell how Johnny saved them from the Indians.

Year-in, year-out, Johnny went on planting seeds. More families lived in the wilderness, now. There were more houses and towns, and everywhere he went his friends were glad to see him.

They asked him to stay for dinner, or as long as he liked. But he would not sit down to dinner until the children ate all they wanted.

One day a boy saw Johnny coming down the road and met him at the door. "Come and look at our trees," said the boy. "They are doing fine."

Johnny's back was to the door, so he did not see anyone come near the house. But the boy jumped up and got a gun. That made Johnny jump, too.

Then Johnny saw an Indian. He walked over to him and said, "I am your friend." After he said some other things, the Indian went away.

"How can you be his friend?" said the boy. "You saved us from the Indians."

"Well," said Johnny, "I think we should help others, when we can. So I will look at your trees, and then I'll go see that Indian. He came here to find me and I want to help him. Next time, why not stop and think before you reach for that gun?"

Many years went by. Johnny was getting to be an old man, but he would not give up his work. He went on planting seeds and took care of the trees he planted.

He liked every one of his apple trees,
old or new, big or little. He was happy to
hear some grandmother say, "Here comes
my friend Johnny. He planted those trees
when I was a girl and it was hard to find
food."

But there came a time when Johnny
was too old to work. He went to live with
friends and many people came to see him.
He liked to tell them about the old days,
when he started out with a sack on
his back, and no shoes on his feet. He
liked to tell them about the old days,
when there were no apple trees in the
wilderness.

New Words in This Book

branch
felt
fight
folks
grew
hard
hurt
Indian
reach
safe
saved
throw
twenty
wilderness

THE SEE AND READ BIOGRAPHIES

DATE DUE